Play Piano with...

John Lennon, Queen, David Bowie, Lou Reed, Paul McCartney, The Doors, Elton John & Simon & Garfunkel

Wise Publications
part of The Music Sales Group

London / New York / Paris / Sydney / Copenhagen / Berlin / Madrid / Tokyo

Published by
Wise Publications
14-15 Berners Street, London W1T 3LJ, UK.

Exclusive Distributors:
Music Sales Limited
Distribution Centre, Newmarket Road, Bury St Edmunds, Suffolk IP33 3YB, UK.
Music Sales Pty Limited
20 Resolution Drive, Caringbah, NSW 2229, Australia.

Order No. AM92009
ISBN 0-7119-4115-7

Compiled by Nick Crispin.
Music arranged by Paul Honey.
Music processed by Paul Ewers Music Design.
Cover photographs, clockwise: Lou Reed (Anja Hinrichsen / Retna USA);
Paul McCartney (Mick Hutson / Redferns); David Bowie (Mick Rock / Starfile);
John Lennon (Peter King / Getty Images); Freddie Mercury (London Features International);
Elton John (Stephane Cardinale / Sygma / Corbis); Jim Morrison (Memory Shop / Corbis Sygma).
Printed in Great Britain by Printwise (Haverhill) Limited, Haverhill, Suffolk.

CD recorded, mixed & mastered by Jonas Persson.
Piano by Paul Honey.
Guitar by Arthur Dick.
Bass by Don Richardson.
Drums by Brett Morgan.
Strings by Dermot Crehan, Justin Pearson & Cathryn McCraken.

Imagine

Words & Music by John Lennon

2 bars count in:

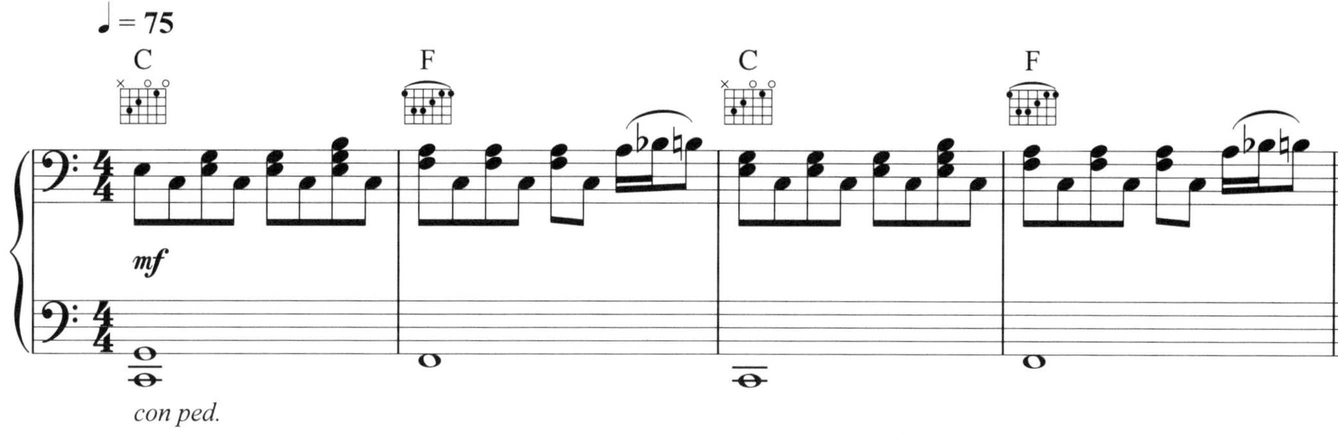
♩ = 75
C
F
C
F
mf
con ped.

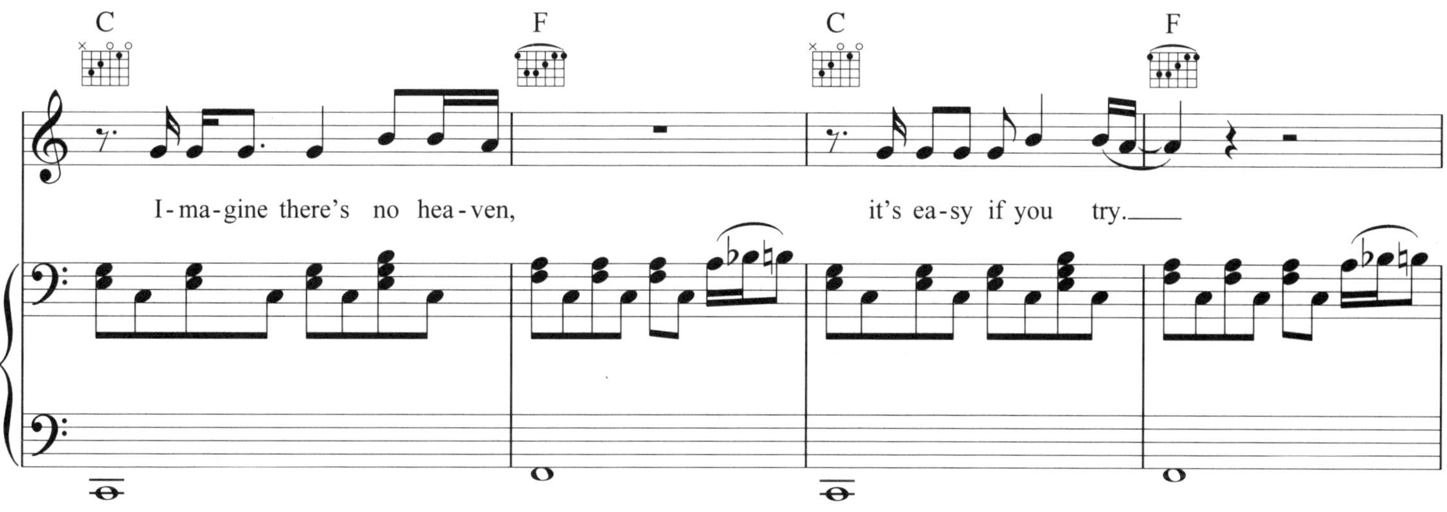
C
F
C
F
I-ma-gine there's no hea-ven,
it's ea-sy if you try.

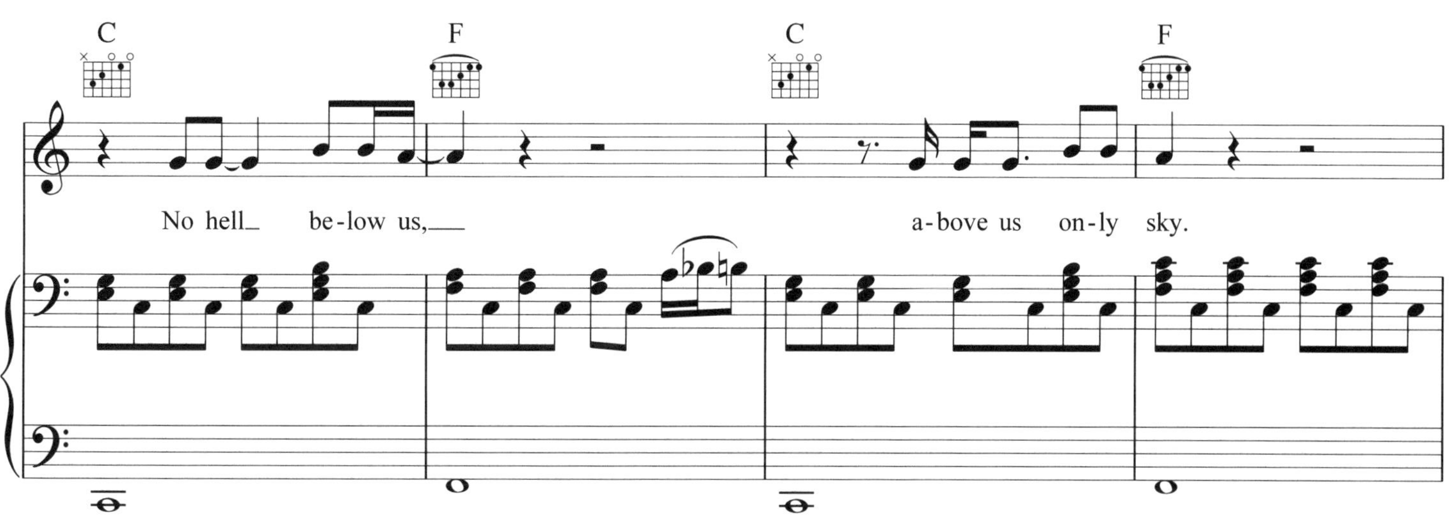
C
F
C
F
No hell be-low us,
a-bove us on-ly sky.

F
F/E
Dm7
F/C
G
C/G
G7
I-ma-gine all the peo - ple
liv-ing for to-day,
Aah.
C
F
C
I-ma-gine there's no coun - tries,
it is-n't hard to do.
I-ma-gine no po-ses-sions,
I won-der if you can.
F
C
F
No-thing to kill or die for,
No need for greed or hun - ger,
C
F
F
F/E
Dm7
F/C
and no re-li-gion too.
our brother hood of man.
I-ma-gine all the peo - ple

G
C/G
G7
F
G
C
Cmaj7
E
E7
liv-ing life in peace, aah. You may say I'm a dream-er,
F
G
C
Cmaj7
E
E7
F
G
To Coda
but I'm not the on - ly one. I hope some day you'll
C
Cmaj7
E
E7
F
G
C
D.S. al Coda
join us, and the world will live as one.
Coda
poco rall.
C
Cmaj7
E
E7
F
G
C
join us, and the world will live as one.

Bridge Over Troubled Water

Words & Music by Paul Simon

A♭ D♭ A♭ E♭ E♭maj7 Fm7 E♭ A♭
when tears are in your eyes I will dry them all.
E♭ A♭ E♭ B♭/D Cm7 B♭7
I'm on your side, oh
E♭ E♭maj7/D E♭7/D♭ E♭7
when times get rough, and friends just
A♭ F7 B♭ E♭ B♭ A♭ B♭/A♭ Adim7
can't be found, like a bridge ov - er

E♭/B♭
C7sus4
C7
A♭
Bdim7
Cm
E♭
B♭
6fr
3fr
4fr
troubled water, I will lay me down, like a
A♭
B♭/A♭
Adim7
E♭/B♭
C7sus4
C7
A♭
Bdim
E♭
E♭7
bridge over troubled water, I will lay me down.
A♭/E♭
E♭
A♭/E♭
E♭
dim.
A♭/E♭
E♭
A♭/E♭
2. When you're down and out, when you're on the

E♭
A♭
D♭
A♭
E♭
E♭maj7
Fm7
street, when eve - ning falls so hard I will
E♭
A♭
E♭
A♭
E♭
B♭/D
Cm7
com - fort you.
I'll take your
cresc.
B♭7
E♭
part, oh, when dark - ness comes,
E♭7/D♭
E♭7
Fm7
E♭7/G
A♭
F7
B♭
E♭
B♭
and pain is all a - round, like a

A♭ B♭/A♭ Adim7 E♭/B♭ C7sus4 C7 A♭ Bdim7
bridge ov - er trou-bled wa-ter, I will lay me down,
Cm E♭ B♭ A♭ B♭/A♭ Adim7 E♭/B♭ C7sus4 Cm7 A♭ G7(♯5)
like a bridge ov - er trou-bled wa-ter, I will lay me down.
Cm Cm/B Cm/B♭ F6 F6/E F6/E♭ E♭/B♭ B♭6 B♭ A♭ Cm
f
A♭ A♭m E♭ A♭/E♭ E♭
mp

A♭/E♭
E♭
A♭/E♭
E♭
Sail on silver girl,
A♭/E♭
E♭
A♭
D♭
A♭
E♭
sail on by.
Your time has come to shine,
Fm7
E♭
A♭
E♭
A♭
E♭
B♭/D
Cm7
all your dreams are on their way.
See how they
cresc.
B♭7
E♭
E♭maj7/D
shine,
oh,
if you need a friend

E♭7/D♭ E♭7 Fm7 E♭7/G A♭ F7 B♭ E♭ B♭ A♭ B♭/A♭ Adim7
I'm sail-ing right be-hind, like a bridge ov-er
E♭/B♭ C7sus4 Cm A♭ G7(♯5)/B Cm E♭ B♭ A♭ B♭/A♭ Adim7
trou-bled wa-ter, I will ease your mind, like a bridge ov-er
E♭/B♭ C7sus4 Cm A♭ G7 Cm Cm/B Cm/B♭ F6 F6/E F6/E♭
trou-bled wa-ter, I will ease your mind.
molto rall.
E♭/B♭ B♭♭6 B♭ A♭ Cm A♭ A♭m E♭
ff

Don't Stop Me Now

Words & Music by Freddie Mercury

2 bars count in:

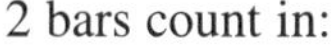

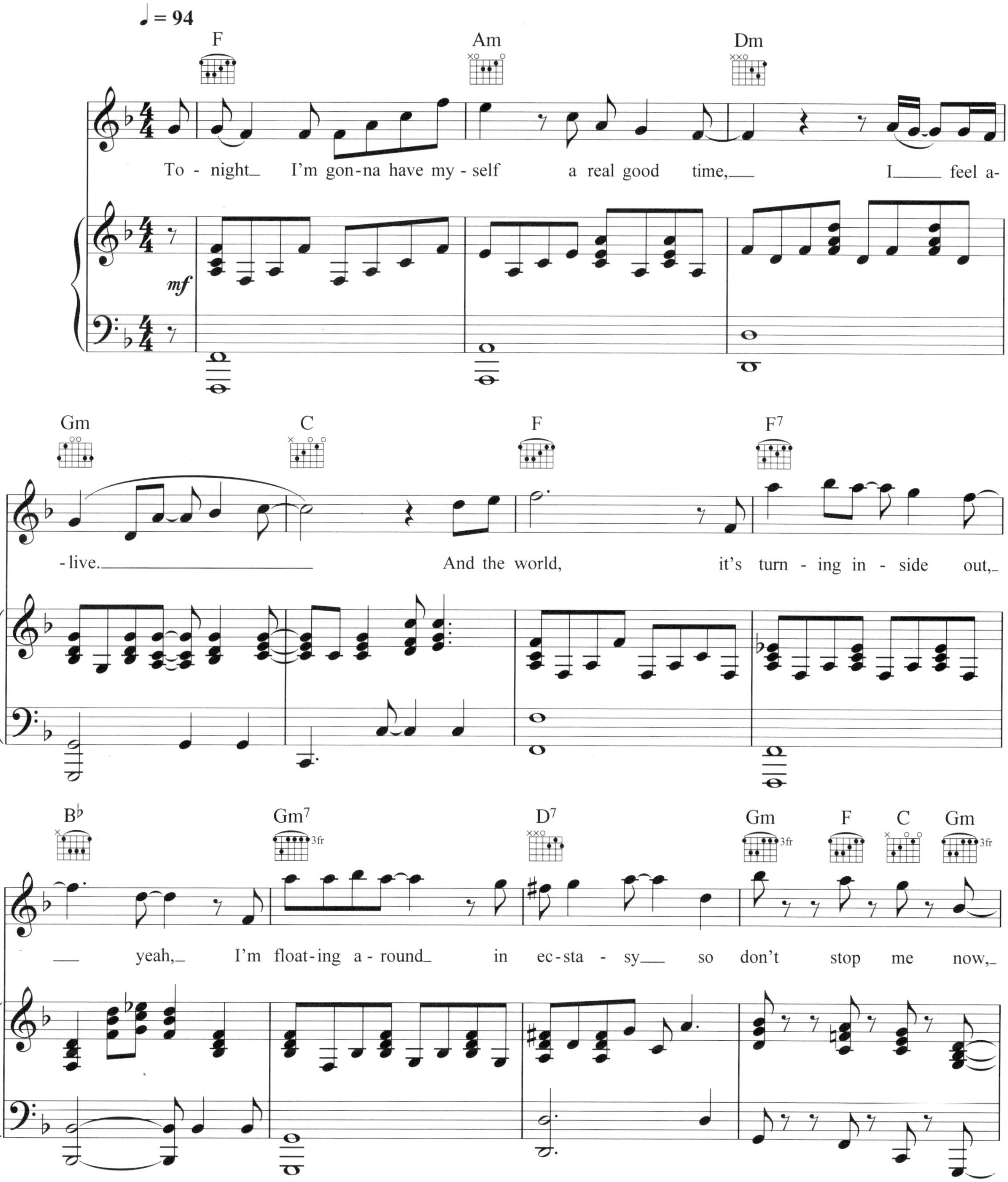

♩ = 94
F
Am
Dm
To - night I'm gon-na have my - self a real good time, I feel a-
mf
Gm
C
F
F7
-live. And the world, it's turn - ing in - side out,
B♭
Gm7
3fr
D7
Gm
3fr
F
C
Gm
3fr
yeah, I'm float-ing a - round in ec-sta - sy so don't stop me now,

Faster ♩ = 158
F
C
Gm
Gm7
3fr
C
C7
don't stop me, 'cos I'm hav-ing a good time, hav-ing a good time. 1. I'm a
f
F
Am
Dm
shoot-ing star leap-ing through the sky like a ti - ger, de-fy-ing the laws
Gm
C
C7
F
Am
of gra-vi - ty. I'm a rac-ing car pass-ing by like La-dy Go-di-
Dm
Gm
C
F
- va, I gon-na go, go, go, there's no stop-ping me. I'm

F7
B♭
Gm7
3fr
burn - ing through the sky, yeah, two hun-dred de-grees that's why they
D7/F♯
Gm
3fr
D7/F♯
call me Mis-ter Fah-ren - heit. I'm travel-ing at the speed of light,
Gm
3fr
Gm7
3fr
C
I wan-na make a su-per-so-nic man out-ta you.
F
Gm
3fr
Am
Dm
Gm7
3fr
C
Don't stop me now, I'm hav-ing such a good time, I'm hav-ing a ball.

F Gm Am Dm Gm7 D7/F♯
3fr
Don't stop_ me now,__ if you wan-na have a good time, just give me a call.______
Gm F C Gm F C Gm
Don't stop me, 'cos I'm hav-ing a good time, don't stop, yes, I'm hav-ing a good_ time, I
To Coda
C A♭/B♭ F
5fr
don't wan-na stop at all.______ 2. I'm a rock-et ship on my way to
Am Dm Gm C C7
Mars______ on a col - li-sion course, I am a sat-te-lite, I'm out of con-trol._ I'm a

F
Am
Dm
sex ma-chine, rea-dy to re-load, like an a-tom bomb a-bout to...
Gm
3fr
C
F
Oh, oh, oh, oh, oh, ex - plode. I'm
F7
B♭
Gm7
3fr
burn - ing through the sky, yeah, two hun-dred de-grees, that's why they
D7
Gm
3fr
D7
call me Mis-ter Fah-ren - heit. I'm trav-'ling at the speed of light,

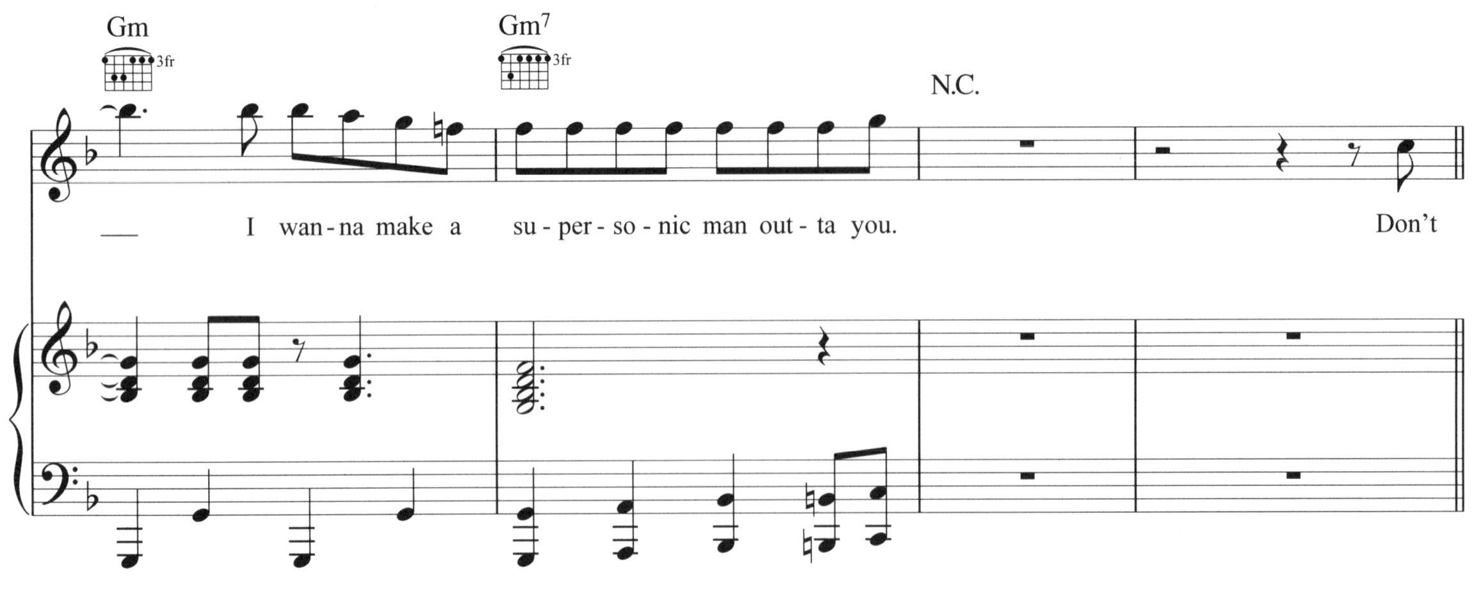
Gm
3fr
Gm7
3fr
N.C.
I wan-na make a su-per-so-nic man out-ta you. Don't

stop me, don't stop me, don't stop me. Don't stop me, don't stop me. Ooh, ooh, ooh. Don't

stop me, don't stop me. Have a good, time, good time. Don't stop me, don't stop me.

F
Am
Dm
Gm
3fr

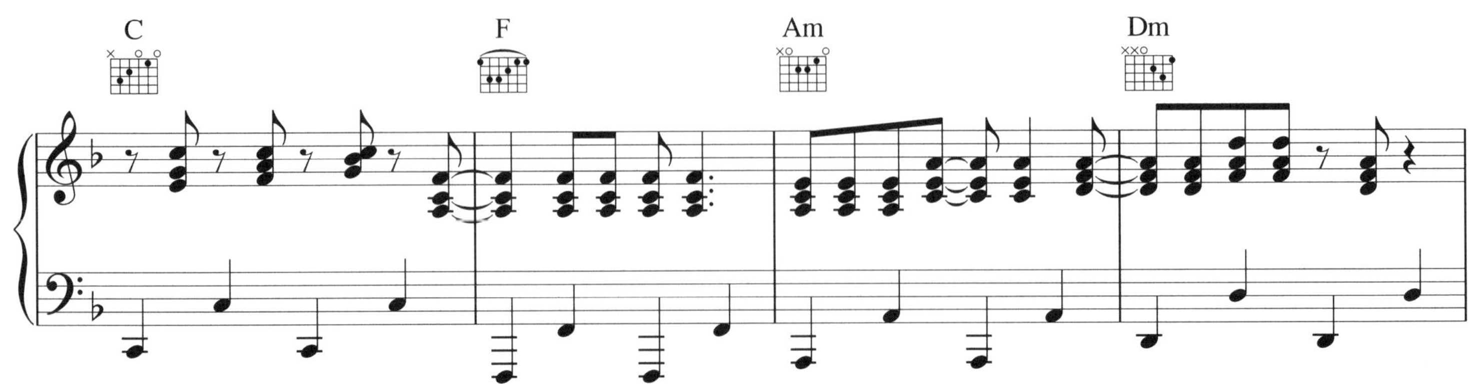
C
F
Am
Dm

Gm
C
F
D.𝄋. al Coda
𝄌 Coda
Tempo primo
A♭/B♭
Oh,
I'm
F
Am
Dm
Gm
Ah,
ah,
ah,
C
F
Fade out
F7
B♭
ah,
ah.

Life On Mars?

Words & Music by David Bowie

Gm
Gm/F
C7
to the seat with the clear-est view,
and she's hooked to the sil - ver screen.
A♭/E♭
Caug/E
Fm
A♭/G♭
A♭sus4/G♭
But the film is a sad-dening bore,
for she's lived it ten times_ or more.
D♭
Faug/A
B♭m
Badd9(♭5)
poco rall.
She could spit in the eyes_ of fools
as they ask her to fo - cus on
B♭
E♭
Gm7
G♭aug
a tempo
sail - lors fight-ing in the dance hall.
Oh, man, look at those cave - men

F
Fm
Cm7
E♭m7
go. It's the frea-ki-est show. Take a look at the
mp
B♭
E♭
Gm7
G♭aug
law - man beat-ing up the wrong guy. Oh, man, won-der if he'll ev-er know
F
Fm
Cm7
E♭m7
he's in the best sell-ing show. Is there life on
8va
mp
Gm
Gm/F♯
Gm7/F
Em7♭5
F
F♯dim
Gm
Ddim7
Mars?

a tempo
Am
B♭
rall.
B♭m
F
F/E
It's on A-me-ri-ca's tor - tured brow
mf
F/E♭
D7
Gm
Gm/F
3fr
that Mick-ey Mouse has grown up a cow,
now the work-ers have struck for fame,
tr
C7
3fr
F
F/E
'cos Len-non's on sale a-gain.
See the mice in their mil - lion hordes
F7/E♭
Dsus4
D7
Gm
Gm7/F
3fr
from I-bi-za to the Nor - folk Broads,
Rule Bri-tan-nia is out of bounds

B♭/C
C
Cm/E♭
Caug/E
to my mo-ther, my dog and clowns.
But the film is a sad-dening bore,
f
Fm
A♭/G♭
D♭
Faug/A
'cos I wrote it ten times or more,
it's a-bout to be writ a-gain
a tempo
B♭m
Badd9(♭5)
poco rall.
B♭
E♭
as I ask to to fo - cus on
sail - ors fight-ing in the dance hall.
3
Gm7
G♭aug
F
Fm
Oh, man, look at those cave-men go.
It's the frea-ki-est show.
mp

Cm7
E♭m7
B♭
E♭
3fr
6fr
Take a look at the law - man beat-ing up the wrong guy.
Gm7
G♭aug
F
Fm
Oh, man, won-der if he'll ev - er know
he's in the best sell-ing show.
mp
Cm7
E♭m7
Gm
Gm/F♯
Gm7/F
Em7♭5
F
F♯dim
5fr
Is there life on Mars?
molto rall.
Gm
B♭/F
E♭
E♭m
B♭

Maybe I'm Amazed

Words & Music by Paul McCartney

2 bars count in:

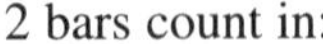

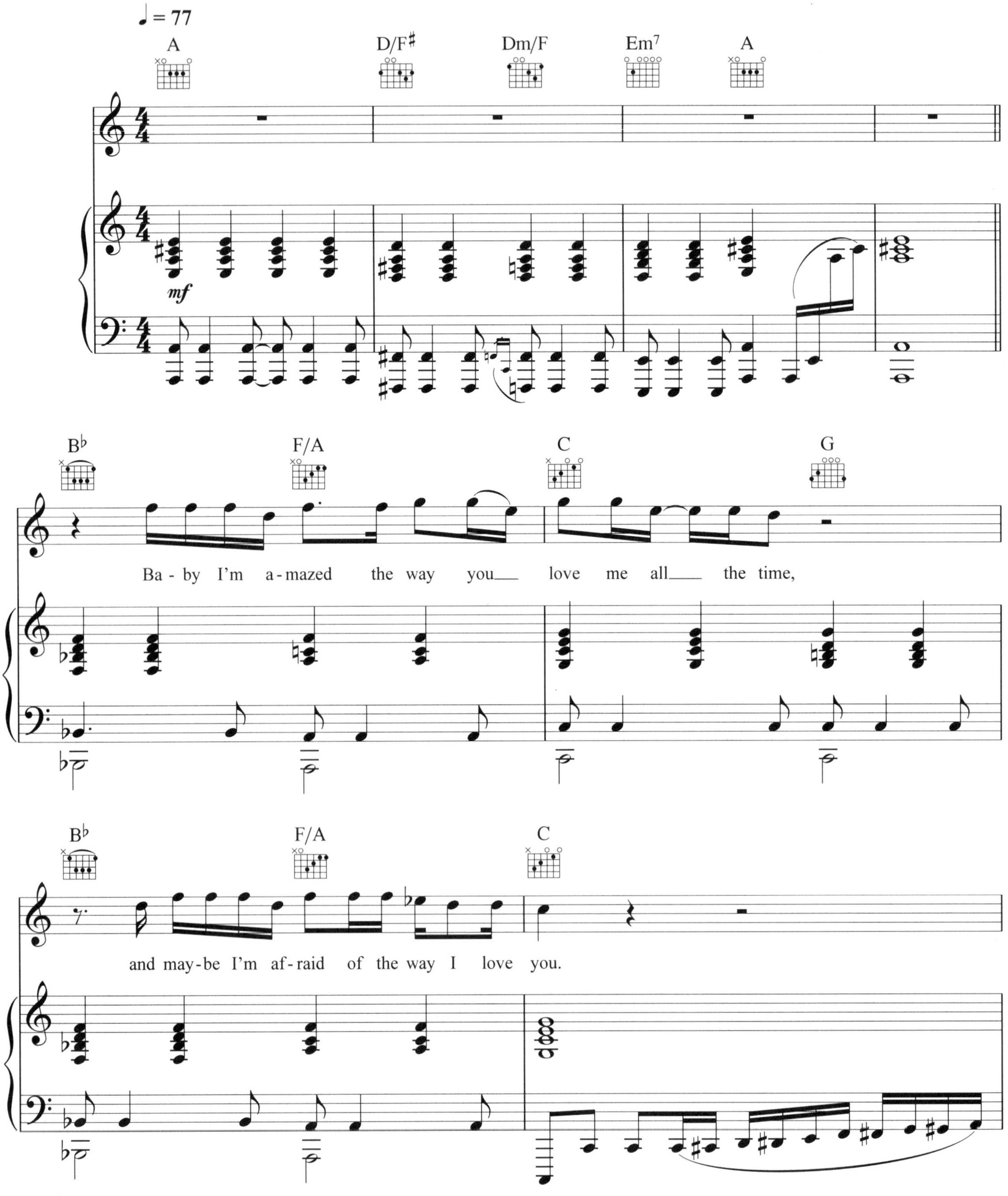

♩ = 77
A
D/F♯
Dm/F
Em7
A
mf
B♭
F/A
C
G
Ba - by I'm a - mazed the way you love me all the time,
B♭
F/A
C
and may - be I'm af - raid of the way I love you.

B♭
F/A
C
G
B♭
F/A
Ba-by I'm a-mazed at the way you pulled me out_ of time,
you hung me on_ a line,
A♭
4fr
E♭/G
3fr
C
may-be I'm a-mazed at the way I real - ly need_ you.
D
A/D
Am/D
Am/F♯
Ba-by I'm a man,
may-be I'm a lone-ly man_ who's in the mid-dle of some-thing_
f
G
D
Dadd9
2fr
that he does-n't real-ly un - der-stand.

D
A/D
Am/D
Am/F♯
Ba - by I'm a man, and may - be you're the on - ly wo - man who could ev - er help__ me,
G
D/F♯
Dm/F
Em7
A
ba - by won't you help me un - der - stand?__ Ooh.
B♭
F/A
C
G
Guitar solo
B♭
F/A
C
B♭
F/A
C
G

B♭
F/A
Fm/A♭
E♭/G
3fr
C
D
A/D
Am/D
Am/F♯
Ba - by I'm a man, may - be I'm a lone - ly man who's in the mid - dle of some - thing
G
D
Dadd9
2fr
that he does - n't real - ly un - der - stand.
D
A/D
Am/D
Am/F♯
Ba - by I'm a man, and may - be you're the on - ly wo - man who could ev - er help me,

G
D/F♯
Dm/F
Em7
A
ba-by won't you help me un - der-stand?
Ooh.
B♭
F/A
C
G
Ba - by I'm a-mazed the way you're with me all the time,
B♭
F/A
C
and may-be I'm af-raid of the way I need you.
B♭
F/A
C
G
B♭
F/A
Ba-by I'm a-mazed at the way you help me sing the song, you right me when I'm wrong,

A♭
E♭/G
C
D
A/D
may-be I'm a-mazed at the way I real - ly need you.
Oh, oh,
Am/D
Am/F♯
G
D Dadd9
oh,
yeah.
D
A/D
Am/D
Am/F♯
G
Oh, oh, oh,
yeah.
D/F♯
Dm/F
Em7
A
Ooh.

B♭
F/A
C
G
Guitar solo
Fm/A♭
E♭/G
3fr
D
A/D
Am/D
Am/F♯
Repeat to fade

Perfect Day

Words & Music by Lou Reed

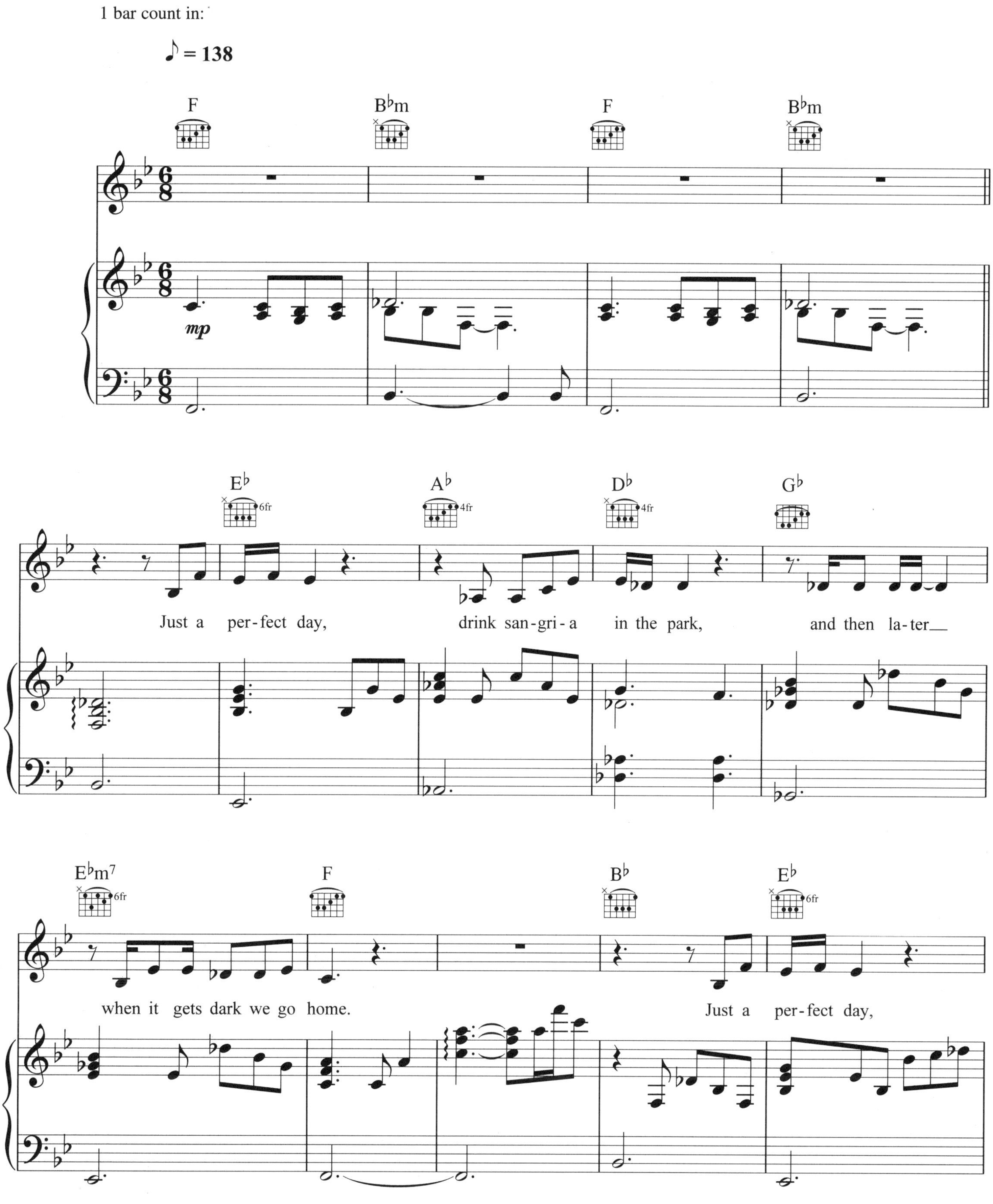

1 bar count in:
♪ = 138
F
B♭m
F
B♭m
mp
E♭
6fr
A♭
4fr
D♭
4fr
G♭
Just a per-fect day, drink san-gri-a in the park, and then la-ter
E♭m7
6fr
F
B♭
E♭
6fr
when it gets dark we go home. Just a per-fect day,

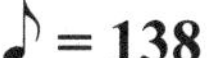

A♭
D♭
G♭
E♭m7
4fr
4fr
6fr
feed a-ni-mals in the zoo, then la-ter a mo-vie too, and then
F
B♭
E♭
Dm
6fr
home. Oh, it's such a per-fect day, I'm glad I spent it with
f
E♭
B♭
F
Gm
F
E♭
6fr
3fr
6fr
you. Oh, such a per-fect day, you just keep me hang-ing on, you just
Gm
F
E♭
B♭m
E♭
3fr
6fr
6fr
keep me hang-ing on.
2. Just a per-fect day,
dim.

A♭
4fr
D♭
4fr
G♭
E♭m7
6fr
F
prob - lems all left a - lone, week - end - ers on our own, it's such fun.
B♭m
E♭
6fr
A♭
4fr
D♭
4fr
Just a per - fect day, you made me for - get my self,
G♭
E♭m7
6fr
F
I thought I was some - one else, some - one good. Oh,
B♭
E♭
6fr
Dm
E♭
6fr
B♭
it's such a per - fect day, I'm glad I spent it with you. Oh, such a
f

F
Gm
F
E♭
Gm
F
E♭
3fr
6fr
3fr
6fr
per-fect day, you just keep me hang-ing on,___ you just keep me hang-ing on.___
Gm
F
E♭
F
Gm
F
3fr
6fr
3fr
E♭
F
Gm
F
E♭
6fr
3fr
6fr
Dm/A
A♭
E♭
B♭
Dm/A
4fr
6fr
You're going to reap_ just what___ you sow. You're going to

A♭
4fr
E♭
6fr
B♭
Dm/A
A♭
4fr
reap just what you sow.
You're going to reap just what
E♭
6fr
B♭
Dm/A
A♭
4fr
E♭
6fr
you sow.
You're going to reap just what you sow.
B♭
Dm/A
A♭
4fr
E♭
6fr
B♭
Dm/A
A♭
4fr
E♭
6fr
poco rall.
B♭

Riders On The Storm

Words & Music by Jim Morrison, Robbie Krieger, Ray Manzarek & John Densmore

Am
Bm/A
Am7
D
Em
D/E
Em
-to this house we're born,
in - to this world we're thrown.
Like a
D
C
Em
A/E
Em7
A/E
dog with-out a bone, an
ac-tor out on loan,
ri-ders on the storm.
There's a
Em
A/E
Em7
A/E
Em
A/E
kill - er on the road,
his brain is squirm-ing like a toad.
Em7
A/E
Am
Bm/A
Am7
D/A
Take a long ho - li - day,

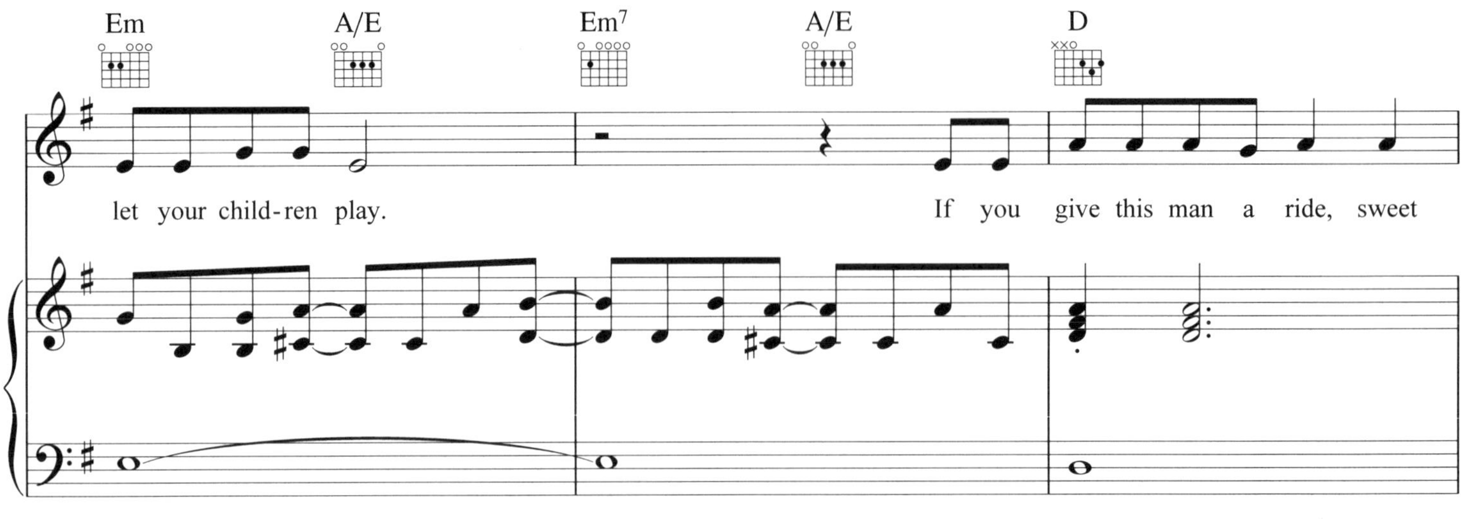
Em
A/E
Em7
A/E
D
let your child-ren play.
If you give this man a ride, sweet

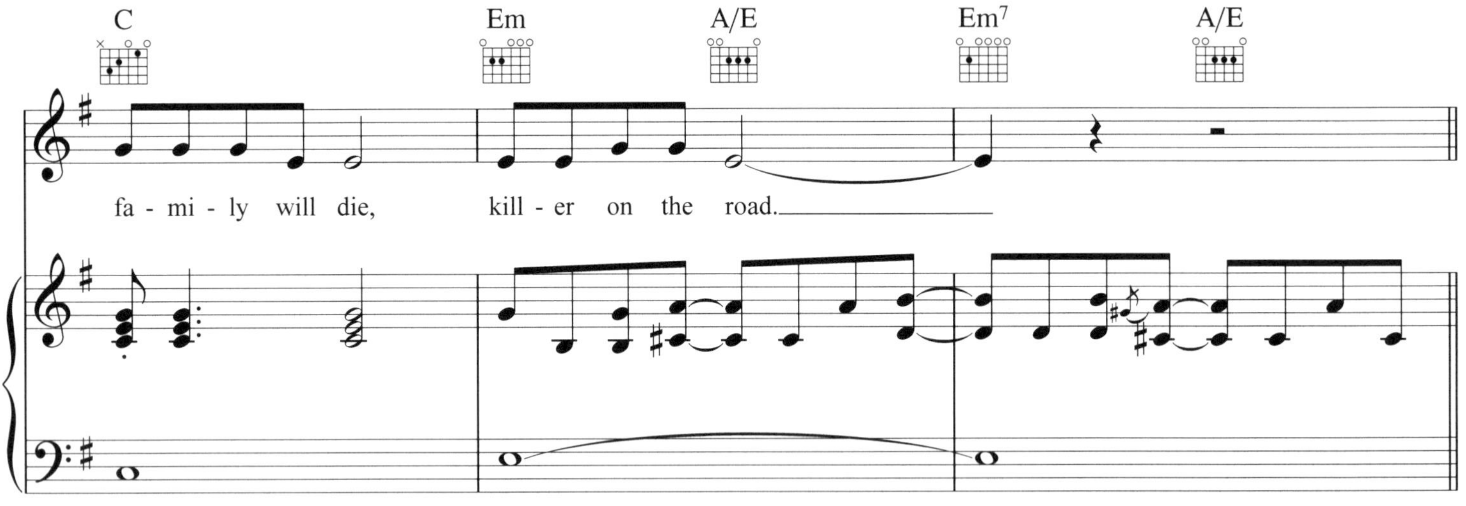
C
Em
A/E
Em7
A/E
fa - mi - ly will die,
kill - er on the road.

Em
Am
Bm/A
Guitar solo

Am7
D/A
A/E
Em7
G/D
D
C

Em
A/E
Em7
A/E
Em
A/E
Em7
A/E
Girl, you
Em
A/E
Em7
A/E
Em
A/E
got - ta love your man,
girl, you got - ta love your man.
Em7
A/E
Am
Bm/A
Am7
D/A
Take him by the hand,
Em
A/E
Em7
A/E
G/D
D
make him un - der - stand.
The world on you de - pends, our

D
C
Em
A/E
Em7
A/E
life will ne - ver end. You got - ta love your man.

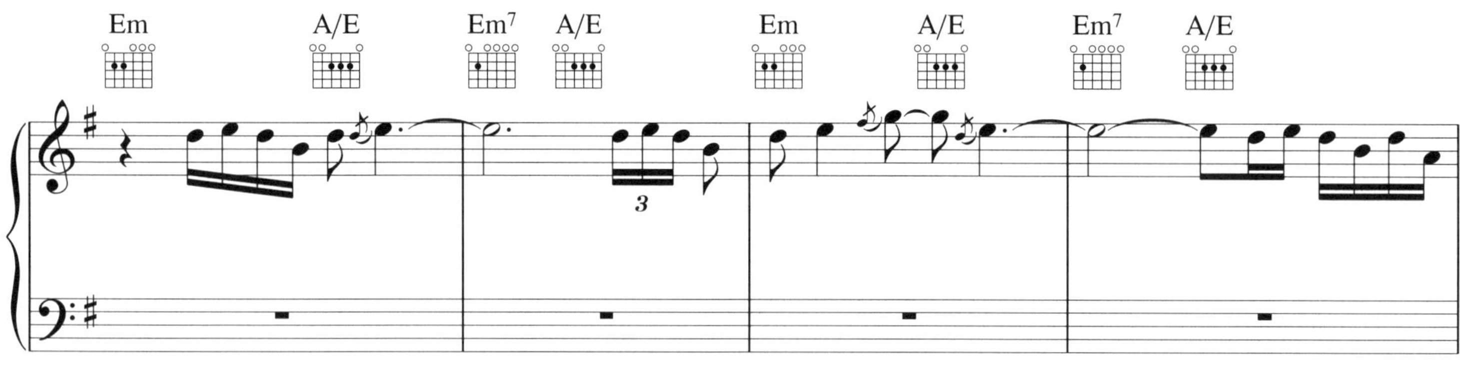
Em
A/E
Em7
A/E
Em
A/E
Em7
A/E
3

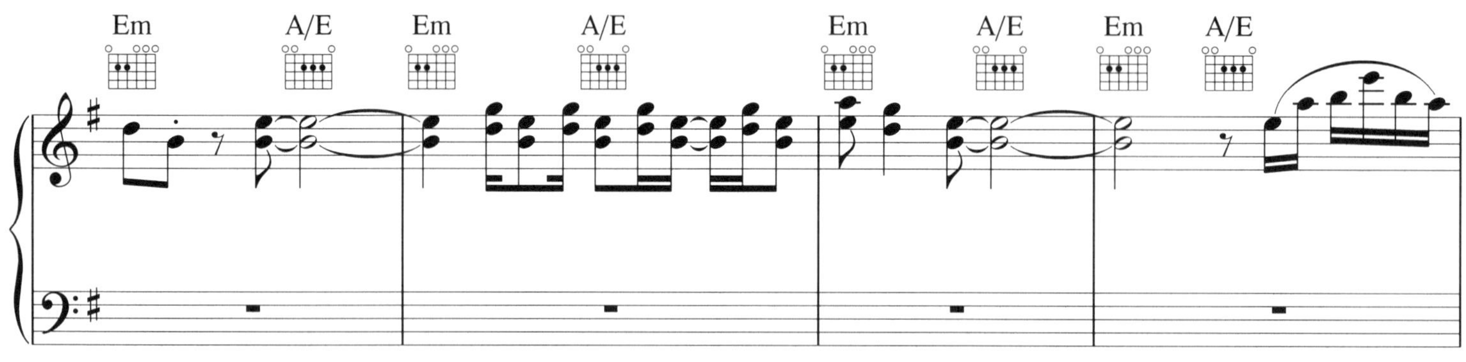
Em
A/E
Em
A/E
Em
A/E
Em
A/E

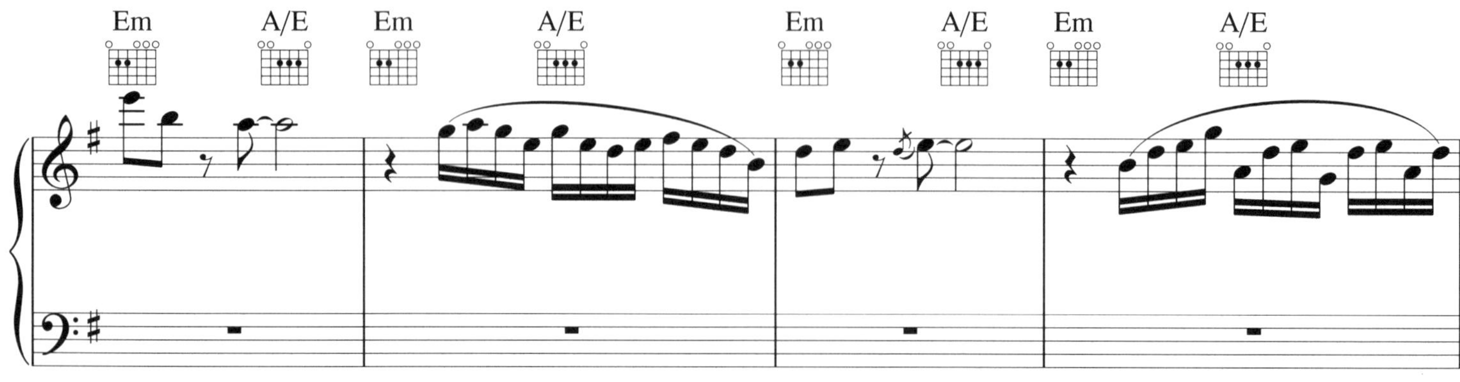
Em
A/E
Em
A/E
Em
A/E
Em
A/E

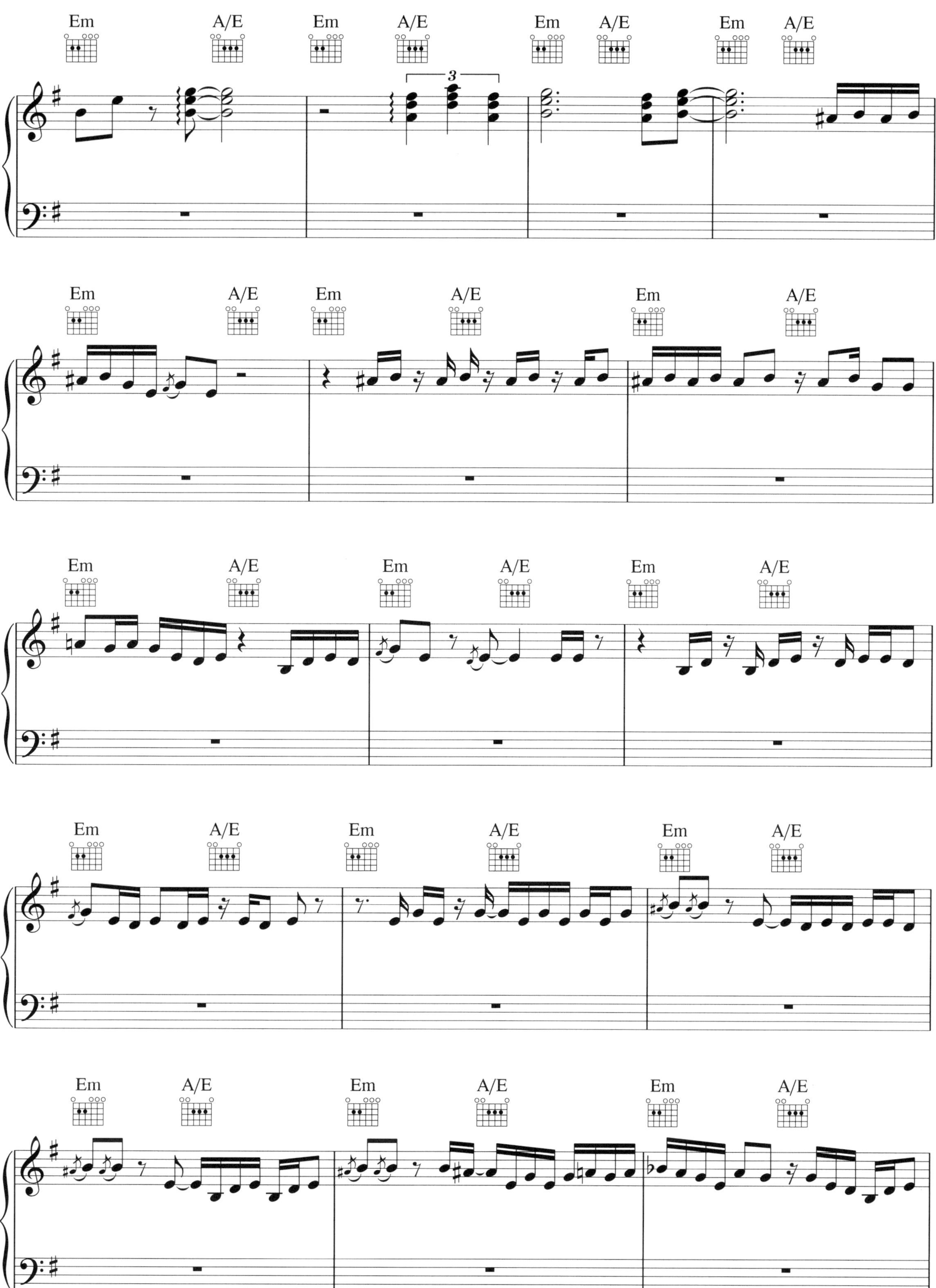

Em
A/E
Em
A/E
Em
A/E
Em
A/E
3

Em
A/E
Em
A/E
Em
A/E
Em
A/E
Em
A/E
Em
A/E
Em
A/E
Em
A/E
Em
A/E
Em
A/E
Em
A/E
Em
A/E
Em
A/E
Em
A/E
Em
A/E
Em
A/E
Em
A/E
Em
A
8va
Ped.

Em
A
Em
A
Em
D/E
Em
D/E
Em
D/E
Em
Em
A/E
Em7
A/E
Em
A/E
Em7
A/E
Em
A/E
Em7
A/E
Em
A/E
Em7
A/E
Em
A/E
Em7
A/E
Em
A/E
Em7
A/E
Ri-ders on the storm,
ri-ders on the storm,
in-

Am
Bm/A
Am7
D/A
Em
D/E
Em
-to this house we're born, in - to this world we're thrown. Like a
D
C
Em
A/E
Em7
A/E
dog with-out a bone, an ac-tor out on loan, ri-ders on the storm.
Em7
A/E
Guitar solo

Em7
A/E
Ri - ders on the storm.
Ri - ders on the storm.
Repeat to fade
Solo ad lib.

Tiny Dancer

Words & Music by Elton John & Bernie Taupin

C
F/C
C
F/C
Pret - ty eyed,
pi - rate smile,
Cadd9
F/A
Cmaj7/G
you'll mar - ry a mu - sic man.
F
Em7
Am7
D/F♯
Bal - le - ri - na,
you must have seen her
Dm7
E
Am
G7/B
danc - ing in the sand.

C
F/C
C
Dm7/C
And now_ she's in__ me,
al - ways with me,_
C
Dm7/C
C
G
F
C/E
Dm7
ti - ny dan-cer in my hand.
C
Dm7/C
C
Dm7/C
C
F/C
C
F/C
C
2. Je - sus freaks,__ out in__ the street,_
hand - in'__ tick-ets out_ for God._

F/A
G/B
C
Dm7/C
C
Dm7/C
Turn-ing back,
she just laughs,
C
Dm7/C
C
F/A
G/B
F
Em7
the bou-le-vard is not that bad.
Pia-no man,
Am7
D/F♯
Dm7/F
E7
Am
G
he makes his stand
in the au-di-to-ri-um.
C
F6
3fr
C
F6
3fr
3. Look-ing on,
she sings the songs

C
Dm7/C
C
G
F
C/E
Dm7
the words_ she knows the tune_ she hums._
C
F/C
C
A♭
B♭
Gm7
Cm
4fr
6fr
3fr
3fr
But oh how it feels_ so real ly - ing here with no - one near,_ on-
A♭
B♭
G/B
4fr
6fr
rall.
- ly you, and you_ can hear_ me, when I_ say soft - ly,_

a tempo
G/D
F
C/E
Dm
C/E
slow - ly.
Hold me clo - ser ti - ny dan - cer,
F
C/E
G/A
count the head - lights on the high - way.
F
C/E
Dm
C/E
F
C/E
Lay me down in sheets of li - nen,
you had a bu - sy day to - day.
G/A
F
C/E
Dm
C/E
Hold me clo - ser ti - ny dan - cer,

F
C/E
G/A
count the head-lights on the high - way.
F
C/E
Dm
C/E
F
C/E
To Coda
Lay me down in sheets of li - nen,
you had a bu - sy day to-day.
G/A
Fadd9/A
G/A
dim.
F/C
C
F/C
C
F/C

C
Dm7/C
C
Dm7/C
C
Blue jean ba - by,
L. A. la - dy,
seams - tress for the band.
F/A
G/B
C
F/C
C
F/C
Pret - ty eyed,
pi - rate smile,
Cadd9
F/A
Cmaj7/G
F
Em7
you'll mar - ry a mu - sic man.
Bal - le - ri - na,
Am7
D/F♯
F6
3fr
E
Am
G
you must have seen her
danc - ing in the sand.

C
F6
3fr
C
F6
3fr
C
Dm7/C
C
And now_ she's in_ me,
al - ways with me,_
ti - ny dan-cer
in my hand._
G
F
C/E
Dm7
C
F/C
C
D.𝄋. al Coda
⊕ Coda
G/A
Fadd9/A
C
F6
3fr
C
F6
3fr
C
F6
3fr
C
F/C
C

7/10 (174857)